KAUAI IN THE EYE OF

By Myles Ludwig

Collector's Edition

An Inter-Pacific Media Publication
Hanalei Bay, Kauai

Iliwai like ka lawe a lilo
Ka ʻĪniki wela, ke ʻĪniki huʻi
    Hahau mai la a lilo kau, lilo kaʻu
Na wai i wehe i ka ipu kapu a Laʻa
    Naʻu ke pani, naʻu ka paʻa
Kūpaʻa a hū ke aloha a…a…a…
    Nou e kalaniheleloa
He kanikau no Kauaʻimanōkalani.
—Ilei Beniamina

This book is dedicated to the brave people of Kauai

Our own heart always exceeds us
—RANIER MARIA WILKE

*A portion of the proceeds resulting from the sale of this book
will be donated to aid the Hurricane Iniki relief effort.*

First Printing, 1992
Printed in Hong Kong
ISBN 1-882709-01-2

Creative Direction: Myles Ludwig
Art Direction & Design: Fred Bechlen, Leo Gonzalez
Design Assistants: Juju Ranches, Stephanie Choy,
Tammy Ebert
Editorial Associate: Chris Cook
Editorial Contributions: The People of Kauai
Photography: Christian Cook, Jeane Dora,
Dennis Fujimoto, Nick Galante,
Gregg Gardiner, The Garden Island,
Ted Hannon, Ken Ige,
The Kauai Times, Myles Ludwig,
Blaine Michioka, Thomas Tamura,
Wide World Photos
Production Manager: Jimmy Tse
Reproduction Supervision: The Hong Kong Studio, Ltd.

CONTENTS

ACKNOWLEDGEMENTS

A project of this magnitude and intensity—conceived and brought to fruition in less than 60 days—requires the assistance, enthusiasm and encouragement of many people.

I want to extend my sincere gratitude to Ted, Mike and Bruce Hannon and Gregg Gardiner for their vision, responsiveness and patronage; to my friend Peter Wolf for his encouragement; to Chris Cook for his invaluable editorial efforts and comradeship; to Fred Bechlen and Leo Gonzalez who were willing to tackle this project under impossible circumstances without sacrificing their high standards of creativity and quality; to all the photographers who responded willingly and quickly to my request for material; and to my long-time colleague Jimmy Tse who turned our idea into a reality of paper and ink.

Special thanks are due my good friends John and Takako Ferry who sheltered me with family and home when mine was uninhabitable and to their children Moana and Makai who illuminated otherwise power-less nights; to Ralph and Sally Rubio and their son Ryan who provided nourishment, companionship and good cheer; to Richard Moore who helped initiate this project; to Patty Ewing and Tom Bodnar who provided me with a bed and friendship on the night of the storm; to Derek and Jan Maitland for their long history of support; to all my friends who sent me expressions of their concern. And to John Michael White who sent us care packages of fresh vegetables and needed supplies to brighten our days.

I owe a special debt of gratitude to Fred Matti, Richard Delaney and the courageous staff of the Princeville Hotel who have earned my undying respect for their bravery, intelligence and good humor during life-threatening moments.

And I thank my family: my daughter Lindsay who survived her own earthquake, my sister Meredith, my brother Seth, and my parents Sol and Muriel Ludwig, themselves survivors of many hurricanes, who understood the depth and seriousness of the situation and who provided immediate, loving support and finally . . . to all the unsung heroes and heroines of Hurricane Iniki, the people who have shown me that, despite tremendous adversity, "lucky you live Kauai."

—Myles Ludwig
19 October 1992, Kauai, Hawaii

The foot
*feels the foot
when it feels
the ground.*
—BUDDHA

Chris, Evelyn and David Cook in front of their storm-tossed Princeville condo.

7

PIERCING THE HEART OF PARADISE

Nature went to war on Kauai on September 11, 1992. It was a civil war; the forces of the heavens locked in mortal combat with the forces of the earth. A war of natures: a moment, as Dostoyevski once wrote, at which the universe seemed "poised to reveal its secret, its mysteries, its deepest truths . . ."

Howling whirlwinds attacked the gentle landscape at ferocious speeds that reached 20,000 feet-per-minute. The very bark was stripped from unsuspecting trees, leaving stands of toothpicks where forests had once preened; proud heads of pandanus were snapped off at the neck, innocent Norfolk pines were brutally torn limb from limb. Man-made structures of metal and wood were twisted with contempt. Tall ironwoods were toppled to lie rusting on the windscorched ground; the island's graceful coconut palms were left weeping.

The sea smoked with fury and raged against the shores, fetching up giant boulders and scattering them like pebbles. Waves of driving, horizontal rain lashed the ancient coastal cliffs, ageing them a century in a matter of hours.

It was war as furious as any fought with the weapons of modern technology. Indeed, when the battle was over, the once Eden-like island looked cauterized as though it had been used as a proving ground for a neutron bomb—one of those that kill buildings, but spare people.

The bones of Kauai were exposed; the very heart of paradise had been pierced.

Bitter irony that the people of Kauai who so loved its sultry lushness, its magical charm, who so fervently sought to preserve its environmental beauty were the victims of this horrific Armageddon. The defenders of nature had become casualties of its wrath.

In half a day, the courses of their lives had been dramatically changed. The statistics are well known: 1-in-3 families left homeless, some 14,000 buildings damaged or entirely destroyed, the population plunged into darkness and deprived of modern convenience, the economy in shambles. But that, as they say, is only the tale of the tape.

Far deeper, more serious scars were left. Despair abounded. The sense of certainty about life was shaken to the quick; all previous *a priori* knowledge was suspended.

Draw your chairs up close to the edge of the precipice and I'll tell you a story...

—F. Scott Fitzgerald

In awe of Iniki at the Princeville Hotel.

9

The proudest, strongest of us were humbled. Shields of wealth and position were meaningless; prayer, faith was our only and best protection.

Was it only happenstance that brought Hurricane Iniki to Kauai? Four times in as many decades the island has been battered by great storms. Tidal waves have left their indelible mark. Could it be true that the island, as some would have it, is a magnetic vortex of cosmic power attracting both the best and worst of the universe? Or had we somehow angered the ancient gods and were being punished for our transgressions?

Yet, science tells us that hurricanes serve a global purpose, aiding the balance of world temperatures by sweeping heat north from the tropics, modulating the atmosphere. "Violent natural processes are an integral part of a delicate and complex environmental system," explains geographic expert George Demko, "and humans in places most affected by them must learn to adjust and adapt . . ."

A blast hit me in the back and sent me skidding across the glistening and puddled floor of the porte-cochere. I could hear my life whistling by my ears; my fingernails scraped along the hotel facade, searching for a grip.

With its name derived from Huracan, the mythic West Indian god of storms, a hurricane is born over tropical seas where winds from opposite directions collide. It is a self-sustaining engine fuelled by water vapor drawn from the ocean. As the warm vapor rises, condensing to clouds, heat energy is released, spiralling upwards ever more rapidly in a chimney-like effect, drawing up more vapor, creating a chain reaction which spews out violent winds and rain as surely as an erupting volcano hurls its fiery booty from the bowels of the earth. The metaphor is complete: lava flows die in the sea; hurricanes die a natural death on land.

Though Iniki took so very much from us it also gave us great gifts. It gave us a renewed sense of the importance of basic values, of the sacredness of life, of the trueness of aloha. By making us feel helpless, it gave us a rebirthed strength. By washing away our superficial differences, it gave us a new understanding of community. It gave us a common bond forged of endurance that will not easily be sundered.

And it left each of us with a story, a story we will never forget; a story we'll be telling our grandchildren, a story that will live for generations.

Myself, I weathered the storm in the glass-walled lobby of the Princeville Hotel. More than a thousand people were sheltered in that building which resembled more a refugee camp than a luxury resort. They filled the ballroom, lined the corridors and hid in the stairwells; all looked dazed, tormented, stunned—ageing by the moment just as were the cliffs of the island.

Many times during those long hours, I feared for my life: when the skylights col-

10

In the eye: (clockwise)
Fred Matti in command;
Linda Hart, Susan
Thomson, Richard
Delaney and others keep
watch; the eye passed
over quickly; Civil
Defense coordinator Len
Prybutok lost his home
but stayed on the job.

lapsed under the buffeting weight of storm shrapnel and debris cascaded onto the marble-floored lobby; when windows trembled and walls vibrated; when doors tied slackly rebelled in anguish against their bounds. When the wind reversed and pounded full-throttle at the corner of the hotel with an overwhelming wildness, I thought I saw in its writhing pattern of air and water, a persona—a face as clear, as angry, as ugly as any one might expect to see in a vision of hell.

When the eye passed over us and the sky cleared momentarily, I went outside to photograph the eerie grayness, the thin, vulnerable clouds floating eastward. Suddenly, the wind came up again and I turned to retreat. A blast hit me in the back and sent me skidding across the glistening and puddled floor of the porte-cochere. I could hear my life whistling by my ears; my fingernails scraped along the hotel facade, searching for a grip. I thought for certain I would be blown through the entry way and over the cliff of Puupoa into oblivion. Miraculously, my forward motion was stopped immediately in front of the hotel entrance; I rushed inside for safety.

That night, driving around Princeville and Hanalei, the full harvest moon silhouetted the skeletal remains of homes and businesses. When I awoke after a short, fitful sleep and stepped outside in the dawn, the pale moon still in the blueing sky, emotion welled up inside of me and spilled out in chunky tears. I cried for Kauai.

It broke my heart...I salute you, the people of Kauai, for your courage and your perseverance. I thank you for your wonderful spirit... Kauai has shown the world how aloha can really work...
—MAYOR JOANN YUKIMURA

But that is my story. If this book had 50,000-some pages, everyone could tell their own version. The tales told here will have to suffice as a symbol for all of us.

A closing note: I have divided this book into sections that relate the terror of the storm, its devastation, the early restoration of the island and the celebrations of life that followed. The last section is as an important record—maybe even more so—as any of the others, because it makes clear that, no matter the damage, the human spirit is alive and strong on Kauai.

The island will heal; it will return to its former grandeur. Some two weeks after Iniki, I was in Kokee with my friend Richard Moore. As we drove up the winding road, a black wild boar scurried across our path. At the Kalalau Lookout, flowers were blooming. We could make out a few goats on the browned slopes of the valley below. And when the mist cleared, a sky painted endearingly by the kind of magnificent sunset we used to take for granted, was revealed.

It was, after all, still Kauai . . . still paradise.

—ML

14

and smote the four corners of the house...
I only am escaped alone to tell thee.
—THE BOOK OF JOB

DEVASTATION

Iniki's fury was unpredictable and indiscriminate. On any given street, one house might be completely destroyed; the one next door, seemingly untouched. Ballistic winds sent roofs flying from one zip code to another, downed 35% of the island's power lines and poles, snapped sturdy trees like twigs, denuded luxuriant forests, and blew away agricultural crops—causing more than a billion dollars' worth of damage.

*A*s long as
we're alive, that's what
matters. People here just
say; Let's get up and get
to work...

—KAIPO KEALALIO, LIHUE

The storm spared no
community on the island.
Killer winds knocked
down walls, ripped off
roofs and twisted metal
around trees and power
poles.

FLORIST
ICE
LIQUOR
GROCERIES
PRODUCE
MEATS
PICNIC Supplies

REAL ESTATE

I'*m very pleased
with how much progress
has been made. The
response is really
incredible. There aren't
really any problems.*

—MARILYN QUAYLE

**Iniki cannonballs
(above) at the Coco
Palms resort. At right,
Randy Stanton con-
templates his next step
in his destroyed gym;
only the bleachers
remained intact at the
Kilauea gym; Lihue
suffered extensive
damage.**

*M*y son called me
from Florida and told me
it was going to be bad. I
was alone. When my win-
dows went, I went into my
closet. I was shaking. It
was really bad.

—CLORINDA NAKASHIRO, HANALEI

**In Hanalei, Bailey
Cunning's stuffed lion
dries out. The view at
Wailua Homesteads
changed and some
Princeville condos were
eviscerated; the Koloa
Fire Station in a
convertible mode.**

The shelter at Waimea High School—the band room—was too full to get in, so I stood outside and watched the winds rip up from Waimea Valley. As I was watching, I couldn't even speak; it was something you know is happening, but can't believe. I saw the Waimea church steeple spinning in the air and crash to the ground.

When the eye came, I jumped into my truck to go home . . . When I got home, I couldn't find the front of my house.

—PHYLLIS SAGAWA, WAIMEA

Older, historic buildings were particularly hard hit; a power pole hangs its head sadly.

25

I was doing active duty for the Coast Guard reserve at the joint operations center on Oahu. September 11 was to be my last day. I had been tracking the hurricane. We knew the speed . . . 140mph sustained, gusting at 165mph when it made landfall. We knew the steep mountains between the north and south sides of the island would act as an accelerator. I could only imagine what was happening. It was a very hopeless feeling.

— JIM PYCHA, PRINCEVILLE

The function room at the new Prince Clubhouse was blown out, as were many condos at Pali Ke Kua. At the Kapaa School, No Parking rules were strictly enforced by Mother Nature.

W
e are just a drain
on the community, and we
don't want to be here.
Get us out.

—VISITOR ANDREW SZASZ

Island-wide damages
were estimated at over
one billion dollars.
Waimea aerial view;
Kilauea home;
macadamia nut trees
downed in Kalaheo;
Kauai Timesman Gregg
Gardiner surveyed the
situation aboard a
chopper from PMRF.

I was totally shocked when the eye of the hurricane came through and I saw the sky through my second story bedroom. I would never believe I'd lose my bedroom. But the most amazing thing was the kokua the community provided. It was neighbor helping neighbor.

—BILL HONJIYO, HANAPEPE

Iniki carved out a new landscape in Kokee, though many parts of the forest were unaffected. First Hawaiian Bank's Walter A. Dods, Jr. and Anthony R. Guerrero, Jr. pitched on to help gather much needed supplies. In Hanalei, the Ching Young store and the Trader Building suffered. The Tropical Taco wagon provided shelter though the house lost its topping.

I couldn't believe the force. We were watching trees fly out of the sky and not come down.

—STEVEN SPIELBERG, DIRECTOR ON LOCATION TO FILM JURASSIC PARK.

A nearly-limbless pine symbolized catastrophe. On the South Shore, Poipu resorts were hit by both storm and high waves which changed the contours of the beach. Below right, the Makai Club on the Princeville Golf Course took a drubbing.

I*niki doubled
the size of our beaches in
Poipu, and pruned back
our landscaping.
Between the millions of
new neon green leaves
and the thousands
of square yards of new
sand, Poipu should be in
great shape when the
buildings are renovated.*

—Margy Parker, Poipu

The storm brought life
on Kauai to a halt.
Modern conveniences
became sculptural arti-
facts; even places of
worship were struck
by Iniki's wrath.

34

We were worshipping and thanking the Lord ... singing song with a guitar. When we stopped singing, we heard the hurricane. But I had peace in my heart. I believe that during the storm is the time to find out if we pass the test; we did.

—JESSE LAYAOEN, KILAUEA

Boat owners sought safety on dry land to little avail; luxurious homes in Poipu were swept apart by the storm's fury.

L ook at the
mountains. The moun-
tains have seen hundreds
if not thousands of Inikis.
The mountains have the
crooked smile on their
faces, the smile a dog has
when you scratch 'em in
that 'just so' place.

—AMBROSE "MAKUHIWA",
WAILUA BEACH

From fine hotel to
humble home, there was
no escape from Iniki's
terror.

I was locked in the bathroom with my family. My back was against the wall, my feet braced against the door after the glass broke . . . all by flashlight. I could hear the condo upstairs ripping, ripping. . .then silence; it was gone. I looked at the ocean through one window. It seemed to be on fire; it seemed to be smoking. I was afraid the house would be lost to a wave. I figured the worst. When Taka and I and the kids got back in the morning and saw it was intact, we cried.

—JOHN FERRY, ANINI BEACH

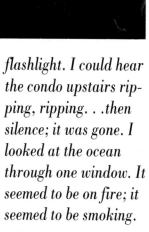

South Shore resorts like the Poipu Sheraton and the Hyatt were hurt by high winds and flooding waters. At right, the morning after . . . the pale moon still in the sky as the new day dawned.

40

RESTORATION

Restoration and relief efforts began immediately. Though normal communication methods were nonexistent, water supply limited, food and gasoline scarce, Kauaiians began cleaning up. Neighbor helped neighbor; the aloha spirit flourished. Within days, branches of the U.S. military, the Red Cross, Salvation Army and the Federal Emergency Management Agency team had arrived to provide much needed assistance in the mammoth task of rebuilding Kauai.

W

e were at the
Kilauea Neighborhood
Center. The roof fell off.
Kilauea Gym fell onto my
car. It was terrifying. I
was too scared to think.
It sounded like we were
inside a cement mixer.

—SARAH WALL, KILAUEA

**Restoration efforts
began immediately, but
it would be some time
before a return to
normalcy would be
achieved.**

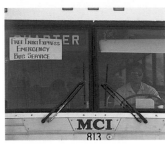

I was scared. There were three of us in the house on the cliff at Kalihiwai over the bay. We moved from room to room, staying under mattresses, as each one was totally wrecked. We ended up in the closet. I thought I was going to die. 'Please, no more, already,' we said. We were on our knees.

—CYNDI PA, KALIHIWAI

The County initiated a free bus service and the military provided hot meals. Many Kauai homes were without water service, so people bathed in streams and waterfalls. The blue tarp became a familiar symbol of restoration.

I was trying to hold the sliding glass doors from blowing in. It was six hours of hell. I thought I was going to die. I felt the wind come up under the house. I thought it would just lift us up and blow it away. I was in shock for four days afterwards.

—C.J. Nakashita, Wailua

Smiling through stress; waiting for the market to open; cleaning up the Tree Tunnel to Koloa, encampment at Kilauea.

Y ou go to the safest part of the house and it starts shaking. You've got nowhere else to go. A piece of wood, about 12" long flew into the window like a missile . . . just missed me. The kids and the women were in the closet with mattresses. Houses on either side of us were destroyed completely. We watched them disintegrate. Nothing felt safe.

—LARRY LEE, JR., WAILUA

Long lines for gasoline were part of life in the first week after the storm. Huge trenches were dug and hurricane debris burned. At left, an Aloha Soldier.

51

I was at my mother-in-law's house; there were eight of us. We hid under the dining room table and covered our heads with blankets and pillows. It was just terrible!

—ADELE MANERA, HANAMAULU

Marilyn Quayle came to inspect; food lines on the West Side. GTE Hawaiian Tel provided free phone banks; a Kilauea family faces an uncertain future; military guards at the Princeville Airport kept order as visitors lined up to leave.

W e hid in the crawl space under the stairs and lined it with futons and pillows and tied the door shut. I didn't know enough to be frightened. I was Cleopatra, Queen of Denial! The worst part was the noise, the sounds, the fury of the wind, the pressure in my ears, layers and layers of glass crashing . . . cacophony. It was life and death. I was aware that I had no control.

—MIMSY BOURET, PRINCEVILLE

KQNG Radio comes back on the air; roofing troopers; familiar scenes.

54

The wind just went blam . . . right into us. Everything went . . . no roof, no ceiling. The walls were breathing in and out and the floors were going up and down. We tried to keep calm . . . we prayed a lot and sang a lot. Praise God, everybody's ok.

—Nani Dosono, Kapaa

It was a happy moment when CyberTel resumed cellular service and islanders could reach friends and family. At right, Gov. John Waihee greets Red Cross president Elizabeth Dole, FEMA sets up shop; phoneman Gary Pacheco works to restore regular service.

56

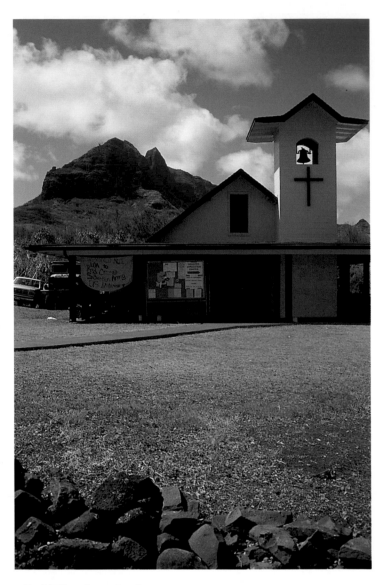

I stayed at the shelter at Kapaa High; part of the ceiling fell in. I was frightened, thought we might die. The next day I returned to look at my house; it was destroyed . . . no roof, walls busted, broken windows, everything wet. I lost everything. I began to cry and kept asking why, why? Why does this have to happen? Now I know there is no answer; we just have to move on.

—LOUISE WORRELL, KAPAA

Crews came from the Mainland and neighbor islands to help bring back the power. Anahola residents found relief at the DAC in a rural setting. The joy of a clean shower in a sparkling waterfall.

CELEBRATION

Having survived the trauma of the storm and the hardships of its aftermath, Kauaiians turned to the celebration of their indomitable spirit. Local businessmen organized and sponsored several "stress relief" events—free, all-day music festivals featuring top local and off-island performers who generously donated their talents to bring smiles back to island faces and express the people's gratitude to those who had provided help. Kauai was coming back to life.

We huddled inside a little cubby hole next to our washer and dryer, peeking out from time to time to watch the wind gather up more speed.

The excitement turned to terror when we started hearing glass breaking around the neighborhood and our big picture window shattered. I peeked around, looked outside and watched the mouth of a tornado cut across the coffee orchard just in front of our house. Had that been a 100 yards closer, our house would not be here today.

—TERI TEASDALE, KALAHEO

Graham and Susan Nash, who lost one of their Kauai homes to the storm, organized a series of benefit concerts which brought together top music stars David Crosby, Steven Stills, Bonnie Rait, Jackson Brown, Jimmy Buffet and Hawaii's own Panuihi Brothers.

We were running back and forth from door to door watching roofs fly off. Then I crawled under a table. My dad kept us calm. When it was over, it was a relief . . . but we were facing a whole new thing—how do we get everything back together?

—TAMARA OURA, WAILUA

Famed duo Cecilio and Kapono headlined the Koloa "stress relief" concert and helped say mahalo to the military.

I*t was one different experience, for sure. Exciting at first, but real hard after. My two kids were real scared, crying. It was much worse than Iwa.*

—ELEANOR HOOKANO, MAKAWELI

Avery Youen helped coordinate the Koloa event which featured Brother Noland (far right) and some happy dancers. On the North Shore, Cathy Ham Young and family gather at Hanalei Bay chill-out.

66

W e were calm,
some of us. But I think I
ate eight meals. I wasn't
in fear; I didn't think
my time was up. The
waiting, the anticipation
was the worst part, And
the last part: 'God, I
thought, enough . . . it
should be over.

—LEILANI COBB-ADAMS, ANAHOLA

In Hanalei, Auntie
Rachel Mahuiki enjoyed
the music organized
by the Kauai Boys' Titus
Kinimaka (right) and
Mike Sheehan, son
Keola and friends.

69

We always knew Kauai was a very unique island, it always stood on its own. Not even Kamehameha the famous alii could conquer. We are the un-conquered kingdom. After Iniki we will stand back up again…Iniki came as a reminder that spiritually we need to clean up, we've gotten very kapulu. When the disaster hit those who didn't belong here, who were using the island as a haven, they left and the ones who stayed are the ones who can make a difference. The true spirit of aloha shows Kauai's spirit to the whole world.

—ILEI BENIAMINA, MAKAWELI

Daryl Kaneshiro helped coordinate the Koloa event; media personality Lee Cataluna was both MC and appreciative audience member. Kauai's next generation gives a sure "shaka."

70

Tomorrow is the most
important thing in life. Comes into us at midnight very clean.
It's perfect when it arrives and it puts itself in our hands.
It hopes we've learned something from yesterday.

—JOHN WAYNE